Vignettes

An Anthology

—

P.S. Clinen

Vignettes – An Anthology

First Published In 2021 By

P.S. Clinen

No part of this document may be reproduced without written consent from the author.

All Rights Reserved

Copyright © 2021 P.S. Clinen

ISBN-13: 978-0-646-83306-4

More from the author can be found at psclinen.com

Also by P.S. Clinen:

Tenebrae Manor

A Boy Named Art

The Will of the Wisp

Contents

Poems 11
- Gull & Leviathan – A Fable 13
- Outer 17
- Amygdala 19
- Lunatic 21
- Greenstone 25
- Caprine Pike 27
- Sower 29
- Harbour (Bare) 31

Prose 33
- Tower of Fog 35
- Astral Trees 45
- Knock Terns 49
- Juniper 55
- To Be a Tree – A Nonsensical Ramble 65

Extras 69
- Tenebrae Manor – Chapter 1 71
- The Will of the Wisp – Chapter 1 85

For B. & Z.

"Amongst the monsters, I am well hidden; who looks for a leaf in a forest?"

- Angela Carter

Poems

Gull & Leviathan – A Fable

White bird, he flew across the blue
To desolation's shore.
'Cross peaks of stone that cloak their bones
with iron shrub and hoar.

About the coast of island ghosts
Did flutter that lone 'gull
He spotted then leviathan –
And perched on living hull.

With water spout spoke mighty trout,
"Why comest thou to me?
My back you greet with combing feet
As though I were your tree."

Stately gull, puffed up and full,
Bespake as claimant then,
"Far I've flown, that I might own
The hills of Kerguelen.

My brothers' song, forever long
Is what I flew to flee.
Their prattling tide made me decide
There are no gulls like me."

Spake again, Leviathan
"Why comest thou to me?
You see me doze within the throes
Of icy reverie."

"To purge that din, a horrid sin –
Birdsong of avian!
Long I yearn for taciturn
Delights of Kerguelen."

Spake again, Leviathan
"Why comest thou to me?
Thy weathered plight, thy feathered flight
Does not relate to me."

"Mistake me not, thou patriot,
I am not here for thee.
I'd thought this place bereft of face –
Alone, I came to be."

Spake again, Leviathan,
"Thou art a thoughtful bird.
How comest thou to disavow
What kin hath ne'er heard?

Fool adrift – go mend this rift!
Do as your kin would do.
Turn back again from whence thou came,
This clime is not for you.

Thy treasure, lo! Thy pleasure, oh!
To be part of a flock.
I am but one, my friends – I've none
Around this dismal rock."

"Oh giant fish, just hear my wish
Pray don't proclaim me rude.
Though here be few, thou knows that two
Can't share of solitude."

Spake again, Leviathan,
"Then thou must leave me be."
Then gull took wing and fish did fling
Itself into the sea.

Leviathan of Kerguelen
Swam round his claimed land.
He'd soon derive birds can't survive
Beyond those blackened sands.

White bird, he flew across the blue
Away from that bleak shoal.
Away from peaks to search and seek
With silent south the goal.

But Winter rose and wings they froze –
Snow drifts but his flock's twin.
And he in white was lost from sight,
Just as he once had been.

Outer

Like the ninth, I watched from outside looking in
And flung towards you through Neptune's cobalt.
The seventh, on its side paid little heed
On Saturn's rings I skate and pick up speed
And shoot past the pregnant pull of Jupiter
To smash through belts of rock and ice
Inward now past Mars – the only red that's cold
Ignoring home despite its patient worry
Into the reckless heat of Venus I yearn
To knock the first from its perch within your sight

We burnt bright and died fast.

My wayward turned head eclipsed the light
And outward bound my course then took the turn
Past home, I won't return, I need not hurry
Even if I wanted, there was nothing I could hold
And purpose sheds its skin and precedes vice
My course but one pulse from the quantum arbiter
And without root I am a useless seed
On the wind of space with vagabond lead
Only faster, no hope of halt
Beyond the ninth into oblivion.

Amygdala

Yggdrasil —
Her full-bellied wax turned to wane

Amygdala —
The shattered shale shifting underfoot
Holding blackened secrets too much for one to bear

Yggdrasil —
Her leaves wilt, her roots rot
And I only helped in cutting the branches
Pruning happiness and throwing it to the pyre

Amygdala —
While fruit and flower were ripped before ripe
And cried out on the ground just out of reach
A broken home with ghosts in its hallways
With poison in its veins

Yggdrasil —
A baby cries in darkness for fear and confusion
Photographs and memories are shoved into a drawer
I've lost all control
I feel nothing, not even pain

Amygdala —
Those aren't your eyes

Lunatic

Sun up –
The lily flowers open sweetly.
The stillness of the day insects betray.
Silent birds perch brooding in the shade;
In undergrowth the sweating lizards lay.

Sun set –
His name young Icarus did scoff.
Bereft the day laments its faded azure.
Tenebrific bats repel the mourners,
Carried off by saintly nocturne measure.

Sun gone –
The lunar crescent petals close.
Moon-scented glowing blossom incubates.
Dancing dryads peel petals anon.
The muse is born, the egg disintegrates.

Awake –
The ancient goblins through the fever
Frolic in the lingering heat of day.
Young dryads drink the stars with infant thirst,
And smell of grass entwines through their array.

Intrude —
The weary traveller staggers lost
And stumbles on this clandestine debut.
The dryads, they did scatter there like leaves
And awful silence permeated through.

The muse —
In puerile scorn did swiftly leer
And left the traveller quivering with fear.

Away!
Her violet eyes aptly command.
The shivering man collapsed and couldn't stand.

Man wept —
And sin became too much to bear.
He prayed, sobbing, for a sunny morrow;
Wept to curtail joy and play perverse;
Wept to see such beauty hid from sorrow.

Where, then?
Could the man now hope to flee
After seeing things no man was meant to see?

How, then?
With this knowledge, could he be
Again within the company of the tree?

Wretched man!
His mind a sword of rust,
Still sharp enough to pierce a thieving mind
That tries to rob the world of mystery
And legend he was never meant to find.

Beware —
To wander in the woods at night
And see the goblins dancing in the vine;
One will see, in twisted, knotted wood
the man and muse forever locked in time.

Greenstone

Fog of the morning gone by midday
Or dreams forgotten on awakening
Stand as memories only in a field
Of carved totems swiftly been
And to turn my head and try to grasp
A moment now in past is worthless
When the green leaves scatter south
And stole no second glance at me
Uselessly I wept with bitter anguish for
Chance and opportune are threads that
Wind a double helix never crossing
As East can never meet the West
I was made to think of eagle spirit
And mindful owls contusing softer plume
Others claimed a peacock swagger that
Could quash the dove's ascent aloft
But truly none could catch the pair of doves
In their rising flight above lands of long clouds
Shaken to their foundation and was it eyes or mind
That saw an onyx beauty, flesh or fabric?
Surely none can know of one when Earth
Has spun but twice or thrice yet maybe
'Tis no different to those whose sun
Has set a thousand times anon
So I drift above a tired midnight sea with
Salvaged stores in mind's eye left unspoken
And maybe we pass like ships in the night

Unbeknownst, our homes at different shoreline
For you were rare as flowers in the Antarctic
And maybe for a moment someone saw you
And maybe in that moment it was I,
I who saw you and did not fathom
What it was I felt when two sides
Of the same coin locked eyes but once
And who was I, unworthy to observe
Such graceful treasure, such a rare and precious jade.

Caprine Pike

Here dance the husks
the husks of men
They dance through flames
they burn to ash
And drums they thump
The goat-skin drums
Tambourine shake
drums they thump

The fire roars
The fire cracks
Like beetle wings

Crack

Shadows tall
The shadows of men
Cinder bespeckled
a dark-led dance
Mottled mothwing
Strangled halitus

This ill wind,
What horror.

Leaves, they spin

In dusk

they glide, they whirl
too dry to rot
To ash, to star
All fall down, to rust
Nothing left
to burn.

There it goes, the dust
There goes the dust
Away, the dust

It's gone

To dusk-woven death
it's gone.

Sower

Little lights on the narrow path
linked together in one place.
See your profile in the shadows cast
never turning to my face.

Shattered nothings falling fast
on a deafened ear.

Pressing flowers in an old book
catching moments that are lost.
Don't you know that they're dead though?
Death for beauty is the cost.

Crumpled under weighted page
in a heavy tomb.

Scattered seeds on the pathway
under swooping of the bird.
Blinded crying in the harsh sun
wishing only to be heard.

Bone broken on the hardened soil
cast upon the floor.

Weakened roots in the shallow ground
seeking purchase in the rock.
Affronted by an indifference
that kept hunger under lock.

Praying for receding tides
and pursuit of sun.

Tangled vines and the sharp thorns
clinging tightly in a web.
Blood pouring and the rust scars
joy of living in an ebb.

Bleeding until hearts run dry
before blinded eyes.

Aching cries in the black sky
only echoes here reply.
Screaming inward from an awful place
where any hope can only die.

Salvation is a lonely writ
in an oblique place.

Little lights on the narrow path
linked together in one place.
See your profile in the shadows cast
never turning turn my face.

Salvation is a lonely writ
in an oblique place.

Salvation is a lonely writ
in an oblique place.

Harbour (Bare)

Away from imbroglios and brouhahas
To the torpid shorelines
Of oleaginous waves
Awash from dread and doubt
Brings forth a pulsing sorrow
Overwhelmed by drowning blues
Of sea and sky and burning sand
Of land-bound winds and crashing wake

In tranquility life is muted

Gulls spin on a mobile
Star-shaped shadows flit across the sand
Concave dune and convex contour
Shrill bell-cry through feathered throats
Rhythmic scuttling under the pier
Careful crab claws collect
Treasures no other would keep
But the high tide who'd steal them back

Stagnant indifference arrests the heart

The ocean recedes toward the horizon
Fish lay putrid and silver
In the stale rays of the day
And the rotted oyster tide
Hulls groan and chip their paint
Their decks creak in horror

Restless convicts of the bay
Knock the lynch-pin wharf

Inward cries split the ribs

Unbearable benevolence
I'd destroy it if I could
To bring an equilibrium
Wrapped in gloom-cloaked wings
She calls my name I am soothed
The oleaginous waves
The torpid shorelines
Wash away dread and doubt

Prose

Tower of Fog

The sun rose, and through the veil of mist, threw its rays with furious abandon at the cloud that perennially coated the mountains. These mountains wound along the bleak coast, corroded fangs weathered by the lashings of sea foam, as stone grey as the sky that stood over them like a loveless parent. They crawled from the earth with the ocean salivating at their heels and reached, reached for the nurturing warmth of sunlight. But the fog remained, the sun set again, and all was lost in eternal monochrome. The northern tower jutted crudely from the peaks, needle-thin, so that the wind that rushed about its zenith whistled like a tuning fork.

In the highest room of the tower, where joviality was given up to the valleys of echoes, Greywaite sat atop a stool. He was of crumbled carriage, as though the oceanic air had weathered his posture inasmuch as the disintegrating horizons surrounding the tower. His white hair receded like waves on a domed beach, slithering backwards from his scalp in lengthy serpents that tumbled floor-bound. Beneath the layers of beard and hair, his cloak bloated about his shapeless form. The navy blue of this cloak, so muted that one must look twice to confirm the presence of any colour at all, pertained to Greywaite's ghostly ensemble, yet added little worth to the stormy gloom of the room. He had waited all night, and now the morning crept upon the tower. The transition towards light was one sluggish and subtle; the overcast sky seemingly dragging the daylight back towards night. It was not as though Greywaite noticed the morning anyway; he merely stared from the window of that airy room out across the peaks to the southern tower that stood in the distance. His eyes were searching, yet old age appeared to have limited his ability to do so. When the yearning for his vision to focus upon the other tower became too frustrating, he turned his gaze to the floor and sighed heavily. The fraying wires of his mind had shot currents betwixt each other in an attempt to comprehend his depression, depression that turned to irritation as a knock sounded at his door.

"Enter."

The door groaned ajar and a figure stepped in, though this figure was somewhat ignored by Greywaite, who continued to stare from the window. For several seconds, there was only the sound of laborious breathing in the room.

"It is you, Flagcloak?"

"The same you would see."

Greywaite turned his head slightly, so that little more than his profile could be discerned from Flagcloak's position. The visitor was of similar stature to the man by the window; perhaps age had been a touch kinder on his rugged features, his shock of hair maintained the golden glow of youth, and coupled with a beard shorter than that of Greywaite, he carried a lion-like appearance. It was from his cracked mouth that the exhalations of a man exhausted exhume, for he had climbed the corroded spiral of stairs to its very summit in order to pay visit to Greywaite. Had Flagcloak not climbed the steps once a day, who else would there be to see him? In spite of the lonesome outpost in which Greywaite perched himself like some crestfallen eagle, Flagcloak, his sole companion, still readily appeared once a day to visit.

The leonine man began to circle the room and admired the dusty ornaments that lined the shelves with a most steady patience. His digits stroked the spines of moth-eaten tomes and caressed the plumage of a stuffed falcon perched lifelessly on the shelf. Flagcloak coughed, for the dust unsettled from some ashen snow globe had permeated his nostrils and surrounded him in a ghostly shroud.

Greywaite, as though only just remembering that he had company, spoke. "I saw him again last night."

Flagcloak turned and followed the aquiline nose of the elderly vulture to where it pointed beyond the open window. "And how did the night fare?"

"My night was…"

Here Greywaite grew frustrated at the very idea of speech, and wished only to tear at his own voice box until silence conquered. He grunted and felt his shoulders droop. His lips parted slightly and from his throat he made to speak again; he fought against his abhorrence and attempted to croak new notes in his birdsong once more.

"As it is every night," he began. "That charlatan. That supercilious apparition – taunting me with its deafness. Every night, Flagcloak. I see that ghost in the southern tower, from the window level with my own. It is but the only light lower than the stars, yet it glows from the highest room of that wicked tower."

"The face, my friend?" replied Flagcloak.

Greywaite snorted, face twisting with disgust. "Ah that face! Staring deadpan from those horrible black eyes. Ignoring any signal of mine to engage with it. Is he so much conceited that he cannot acknowledge me? So long have I sat friendless in this tower, and he mocks me with his staring."

The pair, though not of any conscious accord, switched positions as Flagcloak paced to the window. Greywaite slumped from his stool and leaned heavily upon his writing desk, as though to pour fury from his very beard.

"Had you not thought of going there and uncovering the wight yourself?" Flagcloak asked.

"When he may do the same?" Greywaite retorted, and then calmed. "The perspective, Flagcloak. You do not understand. I have never been to the southern tower. To stand in place of that ghost, to see my dear northern tower from another vantage point... No, I could not."

Greywaite drew beside Flagcloak and gazed at the southern tower, where the window of the accused apparition gaped – a blackened maw.

"A horrifying thought," he muttered.

Flagcloak eyed the old man perplexedly.

"Perhaps tomorrow a change will come," he said.

The cease of speech accentuated the sounds of silence; waves hushed in distant din, and about the pinnacle of southern tower the shrill bell-cry of the seagulls rang sempre forte. Those gulls, spinning as though on the strings of a mobile, would soon drift from the tower and plunge sea-bound with the encroaching night. This Greywaite knew, and as such did not acknowledge them. Readily he returned to the writing desk and allowed his face to droop into his arms – his features contorted with self-inflicted torture. Flagcloak let his vision glass over as the hypnotic gulls sung and glided about the other tower. The light entering through the window illuminated his features – that white and static light held him as a flame embraces a moth.

"The birds…" came Greywaite's muffled voice.

Flagcloak drifted slowly from his reverie. "Hmm?"

"The birds return with the daylight."

With a sigh that shook the dust from his shoulders, Greywaite rapped an impatient fist against his desk, then absently traced the corroded brickwork patterns of the wall before him. An involuntary twitch shivered down his back, and he turned to observe Flagcloak's vacant eyes pouring into him.

"Why do you stare so?"

"Hmm?"

"I… would like to be alone," said Greywaite.

"Would you?" replied Flagcloak.

The two men stared at one another in a seemingly eternal stand-off before Flagcloak broke his gaze, and with little more than a sleight of his hand, pocketed a small item in his cloak – a single match – before heading for the door.

"Until the morrow."

Greywaite did not respond, and returned to the windowsill where the southern tower taunted him with its presence.

Out on the threshold, Flagcloak shivered. The cold hanging dismally over the mountains had not withheld itself from Greywaite's airy room, yet the gusts blowing unabated against the outside walls cut deep into Flagcloak's bones with a new menace. The peaks jutted in serrated hostility, stretching far in three directions. To the east, the sea moaned with the gale, and as Flagcloak began his descent of the spiral stairs, he felt naught but discomfort. The steps coiled about the exterior of the northern tower like an ivy vine, and Flagcloak could not balance himself on any sort of handrail. To his left, the oyster-sharp wall crumbled with erosion. To the right – a sickening precipice. As such his pace was sluggish, and though no sunlight told of the remaining hours of day, he knew he must move somewhat faster if he had any hope of beating the night.

  Onward he trudged, a vapid spectre in the approaching dusk. From his rattling lungs came a wheeze of exertion, steadily breaking with the sound of shore-struck waves. Flagcloak moved as swiftly as his archaic legs would allow, his bare and calloused feet gripping tenaciously against the rocky path that crested the sea cliffs.

  He arrived at an overhang of rock that hid the entrance of a dank cave. Mechanically he took an old lantern hanging from a rusted hook just within his reach. Assailed on all sides by the roar of the ocean echoing off the cave walls, he fumbled with the match procured from his pocket, and despite the moist and loveless air, was able to ignite his lantern. He cast an awful shadow, one hunched and distorted against the cave walls, warping madly as the flame flickered in the oceanic chaos. The sickly orange glow sank further into the cave, until those remaining birds huddled for warmth near the cave mouth were left in the darkness.

    Flagcloak began an ascent as treacherous as that descent from the north tower, fumbling through the gloom up each slimy step; all the while the waters below growled hungrily for him to plummet into the maw. But this was a journey that Flagcloak knew too well. In time he noticed strange shapes forming in his peripherals; a curious light seemed to lurk menacingly outside the range of the dingy lantern, and Flagcloak realised he was close. That curious light was in fact the moon, which signaled his way out of the upper entrance of the cave and up a spiraled stairwell, from which moonlight poured through adorning windows. Round he went, up the steps – seeing now the waxing lunar orb cutting the gluttonous shadows of each protruding stone, and now the inky pitch which consumed the next turn as he climbed the spiral.

    Finally, battered and exhausted, Flagcloak reached the small room he called home. He hung the lantern on the wall by the window, so that the flames contoured every crevasse of his cracked skin, and shadows blackened the globules of his eyes. Flagcloak took a seat upon a stool by the window, from where he could see the distant northern tower, and the hideous figure of Greywaite staring back at him with oblivious hatred.

Astral Trees

It so happened every August, when the year was at its coldest, that the sky above outfit itself with celestial accoutrements so resplendent that the population of Verdigris could only marvel in awe. The light of stars from bygone epochs had finally arrived, and could not but feel, after travelling so far, cheated to appear as just one mote of light on the umbrageous canvas. But to downplay their pulchritude was a disservice to their long journey, and each ornament shone with a deserved grandeur both gracious in its mystery and dignified in its silence. It was beauty unparalleled by any handful of greenstone or malachite, or any lunar blossom of wattle or grevillea; artists would attempt to capture it in their washes, the poets would write of it in their nocturnes, and scholars would piece together the little dots into schematics, as though the night were presenting instructions to its inner workings for them to decode. The spires of the great capital city of Magna Austrinus ascended in the way made clear by stars, and reached in vain from the peak of Cardinal Mons for that which could not be held in hands.

For this month alone the Moon would gaze down on Earth with accompaniment, in this time when the Minor Moon would rise into view from the vermillion dusk to spin a web for itself next to its full-bellied parent. Hereon Major and Minor would embrace in silence with the affection of friends reunited after a long journey, and light up the evenings with a brilliant luminance made possible by the rays refracted off the Rings of Mars. For the people of Verdigris, it was an annual celebration of the cosmos, as well as an admonition to understand a knowledge that had been lost to them; for there were none left alive who knew of that age of darkness – when the night was lit by one lantern – or of the calamitous event that led to its downfall. There were things known and things extirpated, eaten away like a page in a dusty book, and even the most learned of Verdigris' citizens saw their world in the light of an incomplete jigsaw puzzle rather than breaking any new trodden ground. Yes, there were discoveries made all the time, but one knew that knowledge had been gathered up by a previous generation, one that had met an end that scattered all its thoughts and ideals like a dropped bag of marbles – those of this new age were simply tidying up the mess.

    An obvious precedent was the phenomenon known as the Rings of Mars. That curved brush stroke glittering across the sky for one season of the year – the way it rose and set and curled and swept – could only discern that the Earth was a globe, and while the people of Verdigris were utterly adamant that this was true, no woman or man had ever travelled the circumference to confirm it. True, an age of steam had accelerated the methods with which the pioneers could explore, but new challenges always appeared – wild seas, vicious winds, or a 'Land Ho!' met with barren shorelines that were completely uninhabitable. Verdigris was the only sustainable landmass known, and as such, Earth's perimeter was uncharted, its dimensions concealed, and the brilliant reds of Mars' Rings spun silently in the sky, revealing what it could, in the only language it knew how to speak.

    And from below those reds – the crimson, the rose, the coral and cardinal – splashed against the brilliant navy blue of night, on the terra firma of the southerly land of Verdigris, the great minds pondered desperately on those times long past. The maps that remained were enough to spark a childlike fascination – where massive lands were sketched with cities and settlements dotted across them like grains of sand on the beach – a question of how so much of the world had been colonised and obviously livable. Why was it that Verdigris was the only land awashed with life? Why did the trees thrive here and not there, or the waters expunge themselves of poison inland, but the great sea beyond was salted beyond measure? The blooms of the trees yearned to know its roots, to understand that which nourished them, and humanity made its way down the branches of time – some like scurrying beetles, others like dead leaves falling towards a revelation they could no longer share, and the bark of the trunks carved with omnipotent mystery cloaked the enigma of existence, be it divine creation or indifferent accident. The moons knew, the rings knew, the light of stars from times gone – they knew.

Knock Terns

Knock-knock.
The percussive thrum sounded itself through the bush. First here, now there, followed by nowhere at all. Then it came again – *knock knock* – louder this time, cutting through the hazy warmth of the spring morning. The cicadas added their own tremolo symphony; an unchanged din where any renegade sound would be lost in the sonic fuzz. Not a sound, it would seem, could crest that static dirge, until then the percussion sounded again – *knock-knock.*

When it appeared that nobody observed the fetid creek, heard the savage isolation of the insects, or smelled the cloying medicinal scent of the eucalypt (and indeed it would seem nobody did any of these things), the girl charged forward from the shade of the juniper and piqued those artful senses. She broke the tranquil chaos, stood lithe as a panther, eyed the grass in her hand with a magpie fascination.

Knock-knock.

There it was again. It called to her through the rustling of gum leaves, carried its beat betwixt the gnarled agony of Joshua tree branches. The girl dragged a strand of dark hair off her face, coated in sweat, and clasped her teeth down onto her blade of grass. A tooth pick, no - a cigarette (for all the coolest folk smoked) – she would pretend it was a smoke. She breathed deeply of her faux cigarette and found her lungs filled instead with the pollen of wattle; her freckled face contorted, plasticised, and she let loose an almighty and un-lady-like sneeze that shook her body and sent the finches scattering air bound. Her wine-coloured eyes scanned the surroundings – ha ha! Nobody had seen the undignified act.

Whoosh.

No knocking this time. Just the beat of a different kind; the fluttered *whomp-whomp* of wings, as of a bird perching on her shoulder. The avian denizen promptly prodded its beak lightly upon the girl's collar. No *knock-knock,* more of a *tap-tap* on the faded leather of her tunic.

"Late again," she smirked.

The bird spread its maroon crest in retort, before forgetting it was ever insulted and turned to preening its midnight wings. A Knock Tern – and this one belonged to Lucida – an intelligent bird that conveyed messages through some secret language of pecky-pecking on tree trunks.

"You've scratched yourself again, bird," said Lucida, "Silly Nettles."

But Nettles didn't care; knock terns spent their fledgling days hidden in brambles, the thorns warding off predators at the expense of a scritch-a-scratch to their young feathers. He took the strip of grass from Lucida's hand and, realising that it wasn't food, cast it aside with a confident toss of the head.

"Anything?" she asked.

"Caw!" cried Nettles, and he took flight and perched on the branch of a nearby eucalypt.

Knock knock – no.

"I don't believe you,"

Nettles preened his breast, sending feathers drifting toward *terra firma*, while the bird procured a dull brass object as if from nowhere. The rusted thing still glinted slightly in the morning light.

"Ha! I knew it!" Lucida cried, "Cough it up, bird-brain."

With a confidence that one only ever saw in a child such as her, Lucida thrust forth her palm expectantly, her other palm shoved against her hip – like a little teapot short and stout. As Nettles fluttered down to her she recalled that rhyme her nanny had often sung to her, the words whistling through her head in a whirlwind of feathers and memories. And when the dust had settled, and Nettles had reluctantly given up the only possession he had, Lucida gazed down at the corroded cog that sat in her palm like a dusk-washed rose. It was a tiny thing, but no doubt it had once been a vital piece in some ancient machine. She pondered its unassuming façade, personified the corroded scrap and imagined it as underappreciated by other larger cogs. And now the years had sunk their wolf fangs into its sheen, left it to forget its function and disintegrate into the dusk of time.

"Needs a polish," she muttered, and all of a sudden the cog was her favourite thing in the world.

It was a lucky trinket – it had to be; it had found her; she had found it. She would take care of the neglected little thing. Lucida clasped the cog to her chest, squeezing it with such force that it might have crumbled were it more rusted than it was. Dropping to one knee, Lucida procured her dagger from her belt and cut herself a strip of reed growing miserably by the creek bed. No point in rinsing it – the tarn was still, and anything dipped beneath into its shallows would probably come out dirtier than when it was submerged. She braided two reeds together – like her own black pigtails – and looped the little cog onto her new makeshift necklace. *Perfect.* Pleased with her handiwork she rose and sighed; Nettles grumbled from his perch.

"Are you still here, Nettles?"

Nettles had turned his head a full hemisphere, so that his crest looked like a prominent beard. If he understood anything Lucida said to him, he certainly didn't seem to care. The two of them had lurked in The Bush for weeks now, and despite the occasional reference to civilisation (shown, for example, in the brass cog) they had not encountered another human being. Lucida arched her head back and squinted her eyes at the sunlight. Even behind the thin cloud cover the sun shone sharply; when Lucida blinked she could still see the red stamp of it imprinted behind her eyelids. The breeze blew from whence she'd come, bringing with it the hope of a purpose, whispering through the gum leaves and exposing their white-green undersides. The finches cried softly but sternly – even they knew their role, and as Lucida spied a lazy lizard languishing on a warm rock she realised all at once that she was so alone. The heroes had already scoured this land; there was nothing left to discover. She was too late to work the mines that sat abandoned in The Bush; they too had been scavenged for all their worth by the men who, taking their profits, had marched back to The City with a swag of fortune, leaving nothing behind but the by-products of their labour. A cart here, a steel rail warped by heat and moisture – time had left Lucida behind, even though the discovery she longed to experience lay rooted in the past.

"Nettles," she repeated, less sure, "are you still here?"

During her daydream the bird had taken to scratching at the ground with his talons, and once hearing the uncertain sadness in his master's voice he raced to her shoulder and nuzzled her with an animal absence. He might not have understood her 'people' emotions, but there was enough in common betwixt the two creatures for him to comprehend her need for company at that moment. Lucida managed a smile and thought of family, of friendships; there weren't many left, but at least she had her Knock Tern, her wandering feet, her unending thirst for adventure.

"The Steppe must be close," said Lucida, "might see things a bit clearer from there."

Nettles tapped once on her shoulder, *yes*.

"Spring follows Winter, remember what nanny said?"

Knock — yes.

With that the bird took off, his crest a bloodstained streak through the canopy, then gone, but not for long. Lucida knew he'd return once he had found something; for Spring indeed followed Winter, and Lucida's longing for a deserved Summer could, for all she knew, have been closer than ever.

Juniper

Author's note: this poem is taken from my novel **Tenebrae Manor**, *yet, given its unique nature, it can stand alone as its own work. For brief context, a demon named Bordeaux travels across an unknown land in search of a darkness he calls his home.*

Bordeaux had turned back towards the town and readily felt his mind unravel;
after the hours had gone by in thought, he sought a useful way to travel.
To return somehow to his immemorial home and save his friends in time,
He would need to cover ample ground swiftly and the best way would be equine.
Atop a horse's hasty flight of hooves, he would be able to spread his wings
And hope against helplessness that his soaring would fling
Him in the correct direction, the accurate degree of the compass where his home
Waited in mid-peril for him, their saviour, to return from his unexpected roam.
So, within the harbour town, he made his way through the bustling parade
Of markets and stalls and found a merchant with whom he attempted to strike a trade.
Though they spoke no common tongue, Bordeaux's remaining coins and a silver ring,

One of many he wore, were an absolute bounty to the peasant, who stood grinning.
He was more than ecstatic to acquire such treasure for a common horse
And Bordeaux was pleased that his exchange had not required force.
Thus, the crimson demon rode away from the coast and left
The harbour town betwixt the sea and mountains in that salty cleft
Where land and sea locked in embrace. The road he had chosen became
Little more than dust and grass until he found the path had dissipated into no more than a plain.
The sunlight shone down onto his back, igniting the steppe of reeds and flowers
With a vibrant fluorescence of colours – green, blue, yellow and they showered
Onto him, with the foreign intrusive red of his hair and his horse with a pelt of auburn
Disrupting the harmony of those glowing colours poured from the sunny urn.
The breeze whispered sea-bound and flew over his shoulders,
Fleeing the steppe that lay littered with blossomed bud and boulder.
And this wind was accompanied by the glassy currents of the rivers
That ran like veins towards the heart, the sea, in glossy cool slivers.

Breaking the field of verdant green, those trees that stood few and far between
Were of a variety of juniper and Bordeaux had forgotten how open space could spark the serene.
Yet even with such velvet verdancy stretching towards his every horizon,
Each day that passed punctured his confidence and mounted his wizened
Appearance into something increasing haggard and poor;
A weather beating proven by the stubble that sprouted on his gaunt jaw.
Gradually the scene shifted, before eventually growing stale in his heart.
The open space of the fields that once thrilled him did start
To evoke loneliness akin to the forest that he yearned for in vain.
Gone was the freedom of riding across this lush and uninhibited terrain.
All that remained in its place was a crippling and desperate despair
That was magnified verbatim by the roaring rush of the lilies and above, the daylight glare.
Night had revived Bordeaux time and again, so that he pressed
On further until the steppe grew in shoots of tree and became woods. He addressed
The reality of his stark situation. Another change of scene and no hint for him to grope.

He found he was blindly reaching at the fraying strands of his hope.
"I am at a loss. My efforts are futile. I cannot continue on this way," he said.
"I've no idea where my home is and surely my friends may have already assumed me to be dead.
Is there any point to travelling further degrees of longitude on this planet?
Though where else can I go and live in tranquillity unmet?"
Just as Bordeaux had begun giving up and thought he might cast
His anchor overboard, so to speak (for he felt like a rudderless boat) and avast
His travelling for favour of aimlessly drifting alone over the lands,
A certain movement of a creature, namely a tamely colt, captured his glance.
The beast, clearly domesticated, peered from his timid eyes
Beneath the drape of a brush, whose blue-black cones and grey-green fronds disguised
It in a considerable camouflage to the unobservant eye. Although hardly an unusual sight,
The horse made Bordeaux realise a possible end to his plight.
For the wayward appearance of this particular saddled thing could only mean
That a settlement, be it farm or town nearby, would break the monotonous bush land green.

Bordeaux forced his horse into a trot and rounded a corner of hill,
And there, just out of sight down the foot of the slope was a windmill.
It stood as a beacon, towering over the small farmhouse next to it.
The fields of trimmed grass surrounding were inviting, he had to admit.
Straddled by a veranda, the house appeared ancient and in need of repair
And Bordeaux wondered whether its inhabitants still lived there.
As he drew nearer, he dismounted his horse and crept
Towards the flimsy fence near the house. On a sudden his heart leapt,
For the movement of a human being startled Bordeaux.
As she glided from the door of the cottage into the afternoon glow.
The lass he observed was in the prime of youth, simply adorned in a sky-coloured dress.
Her entangled hair glowed a palette of auburn, shifting shades with the sunlight's caress.
As she hung out linen to dry in the sun, Bordeaux attempted to call out and speak.
The travelling had him worn with fatigue and a nagging hunger made him weak,
But could there be harm in confiding with her? There was no town for miles,

This Bordeaux knew, so perhaps she could offer safe lodgings for a while.
So, a demon posed as a man called out at the girl, who showed little shock
At the sudden arrival of a stranger. A turn of her head and a sway of her frock
Preceded a confident smile that startled him; for the ease of her beauty was akin to a nymph
Or any of those other mysterious dryads that hover through nature as sprightly glyphs.
As though he were little more than another tree in the forest, another post in the fence, she turned
And left him alone in the grass. The screen door closed and the wind was all that could be heard.
She returned, with a tan-furred dog at her feet that raced at Bordeaux, whose fearing eyes suddenly bulged wide.
But the dog's advance was friendly and when he looked up again at the girl, she beckoned him inside.
Bordeaux was never quite certain whether the girl spoke a foreign language or simply didn't talk at all
But never once did the girl say a word and her spritely mystery kept the demon in thrall.
Despite the lack of verbalism in their commune, Bordeaux spoke to her often and felt she still understood
The desperation of his situation. He named her Juniper, for the abundance of such plants in the surrounding woods.

Together, they tended to the health of the horse
that had transported Bordeaux safely until now
And as the days drifted by in sweetly, Juniper
carried about her errands feeding chickens and
milking cows.
He had thought that Juniper must live alone;
though found soon enough that she had her own
demons.
In a certain sunny room of her humble house sat
an invalid old man, who painfully cried for deathly
haven.
The man must have been Juniper's father; he
could not stand on his own accord.
He was completely dependent and the man's tears
were his only way of expressing thanks to his
ward.
The sight of the sickly man struck a chord in
Bordeaux's heart
And he tried to ask Juniper how she became tied
to this part.
It seemed to upset the girl to reminisce, she
showed Bordeaux a grave
That stood lonely at the bottom of the garden, at
the back of the enclave.
With the headstone unmarked, Bordeaux could
not discern whom the grave was for
But gathered it must have been her husband or
mother, someone else who may have poured
Their heart into the tending of this farm and the
caring of the sick old man.

Bordeaux realised that Juniper too, was trapped in a world of limited span.
As the sunlight filtered through the quiet days, he felt his heart become enveloped
With fires of love and tenderness, albeit somewhat impetuous and less developed.
Perhaps it was merely the farmland's secluded reality presenting idea of freedom
Or that Juniper represented the folklore of more relatable kingdom.
Their similarities were unassailable; she too was stuck in a world reliant on her servitude,
So maybe between them, they could share their inequitable load and belay the attitude
Owing to a life where their whims, fancies and dreams would always be second
To the needs of others that lay languid in their introspective pond.
Yet these very thoughts ended up pivotal and soon Bordeaux's calling took its toll.
He realised that he was chasing an ideal life that he could never hope to control.
Although in his heart, he felt that staying with Juniper was no act of whim,
Nothing would change the fact that his own home and friends needed him.
The emotion welled in his chest and when he one day caught Juniper's gaze,
He exclaimed, "Juniper, this cannot work! I cannot stay. Though your beauty amaze,

You don't understand the words that I say and
nor could I hope to properly know you.
Even though the agony we feel is certainly
burdened well together, you know it to be true!
Between us there is mutual devotion, derived of
my love of your heart, so altruistic!
No chimera could destroy my knightly ambition
to nurture you, my fantastic!
But while my home calls for me, the idea of us
united is indeed a chimera,
Aspired dream must give way to my responsibility,
such cruel terror!
Oh chimera – a dream from whence I stumble on
my words, darling Juniper.
Let me say – no other muse compares to you, you
star of brighter luminance than Jupiter."
Juniper's eyes swelled with a torrent of tears as she
clutched at her heart.
The deluge of Bordeaux's avowal, even with their
foreign linguistics, did impart
The expression intended. And her acceptance of
his pleas shone through their mutual affection,
The realisation that both must go alone and attend
to their own afflictions.
He longingly stared at her with sorrowful eyes and
repeated, "I have to go."
Juniper kissed him softly on the cheek and
whispered a word for him, "Bordeaux."
His horse was prepared in the symphonic
nocturne of the evening, where the crickets

Rung their ornamental anthem sempre forte in the gnarled brambly thickets.
Bordeaux painfully uttered farewell and hoped to guide himself through the treacherous shoals
With the spritely image of Juniper forever etched into his soul.

To Be a Tree – A Nonsensical Ramble

If I were to be a tree, only a few pressing concerns would plague my petiolar mind. Foremost being the present equilibrium (or lack thereof) between rain and sunshine at any given moment, short of the random yet necessary question of how cold one's branches would feel in the wintertime with no appropriate coverage of foliage to protect. For the latter, concern is easily abated with the decision that I would be an evergreen. Assessing and acknowledging these risks, I adamantly pronounce that I want to be a big, huge tree.

  If I were to be a tree, what power would brim in my sturdy trunk, as I stand tall against fierce gales of mid-December proportions. As gusts of nature's howling voice rush around my presence as a high tide wave would an anchored rock. Such tenacity flowing through my unyielding roots, only increased by the absorbing of nutrients from the delightful soil at my entangled feet. Draining the earth dry of its molten middle, as it were, to an empty husk.

  If I were to be a tree, what joy discerned by avian allies acquainting their feathery quills to my symphonic leaves. Loquacious arias alighting from coloured birds coinciding with the passing or arriving of the sun, drifting from promising aubade to melancholic nocturne. To cradle the fragile eggs amongst burly branches in pouches constructed of my lesser arms (my fingers, one might call them, though I suppose most refer to them as twigs). A provision for utmost care, camouflaging said birds from harm's punish – and soon! These freckled medallions crack and keel away to reveal the latest of my choir, young falsettos of immature urgency, answered in turn by the baritones and tenors of their paternal superiors.

If I were to be a tree, (pertaining to plant law, as I'll call it) I would oft be branded to the colour of green. This certain detail sits contentedly in my mindset, as green just so happens to be my favourite colour. My leaves, numbering a mere seven hundred and eighty-three during the most frigid of winters, and a boom two hundred and sixty-three thousand nine hundred and forty-one during the most vibrant of summers, would be the major showcase for my spectral quality. Green of four instantly noticeable shades and the shapes of stars, blades, hands and in one case, a half-closed eye with enormous pupil, thanks to a gluttonous caterpillar feasting upon it.

If I were to be tree, how sombre I'd become reminiscing of friends gone, taken from me with each rotation of celestial sphere. Of bugs and birds and butterflies gone perished with the preceding months, to flowers and grass and hanging ivy slain by time's sword. Yet still I'd stand on eternal, ever watchful, a beacon of antiquity. As the youths who climb my branches become couples who carve messages in my outmost layer of bark encumber my still existence; those who share my shade and stare skyward through the canopy of leaf constellations, broken only by filtering sun that pierces through in sceptres of light. And all the while the dryads dance between leaves in sprightly joviality.

      Yes, if I were to be a tree, how similar life would be to that of what I am now. Although a life with no pulse, there is a life with joy, with observation, with friends and in loneliness. A life with a beginning and a life with an end. But should I pursue my ambition to become such a ligneous denizen, my progress would swiftly be extinguished by the simple fact that for a man to become a tree, one would have to defy all notions of sense and reality, it is perfectly impossible!

Extras

Tenebrae Manor – Chapter 1

The following pages contain the first chapter of ***Tenebrae Manor*** – the debut novel of P.S.Clinen.

Within uncharted forest, where ancient magic keeps the night sky ever-present, stands Tenebrae Manor. Within its dusky walls dwell beings of macabre whimsy, headed by the pedant demon, Bordeaux, and the hedonistic gorgon, Lady Libra. These apparitions are content to live out their eternity in the half-lit gloom; that is until the arrival of a certain uninvited guest – a live human being – imperils the concealment of Tenebrae Manor and the livelihood of its residents. And in the forest surrounding a new threat emerges – a threat that is rattling the once still trees, and dooming the manor towards irreparable decay. But the characters are unmoored. While some seem desperate to maintain ascendancy over their ruinous home, others adopt a façade of mischievous indifference that could undo them all. And is Tenebrae Manor even worth saving? After all, eternity is a frightfully long time to spend alone...

Bordeaux Speaks with Crow

The epochs pass. A certain higher-sensed creature records its progress. And though a time has been reached where this creature can safely assume that all has been revealed to him – namely that modern man has tread upon all the earth, certain locales have been deemed but futile to the progression of his culture. As such, there are places dotting the planet that have remained ignored for centuries. One such region exists somewhere where coniferous forest and unyielding rock have deemed exploration and habitation impossible. Lost among these mountains, seemingly teetering on the edge of the world itself, stands Tenebrae Manor. Pertaining to the architectural calibre of styles introduced centuries apart, the mansion dons an immediately unique and timeless appearance. Upon observing characteristics seen on the ancient keeps of the dark ages, to whimsical features native of Georgian and Gothic decor, it is at once discernible that Tenebrae Manor must have stood for centuries. But the epochs pass, and that umbrageous façade remains untouched by the populace, merging into a sort of sickly castle-mansion hybrid. The uninviting mansion is home to a handful of surreal apparitions, doting the darkness with twilit minds set only on utter seclusion from the outside world around them. They are a ghastly bunch, floating aimlessly down the endless dusty corridors.

Who are these beings? These immortal wights of a half-lit world? They are like the centipedes that scurry about their way in the soiled gloom as anti-supernal apparitions, avoiding the ways of the vagabond through strict adhesion to their immemorial home. Through a torrent of time so punishingly unrelenting, yielding not to the bemoans of ennui, of stagnation, these vapid spectres of shadow trudge ever onward. Adrift as they are in the vast cosmical sea of tree and rock, they gather. They gather because there is no one else. There is nothing else. This is the world they know, the world so omnipresent that any previous memories of a life before have been lost to the swampy recesses of the mind - like old dreams that one almost certainly forgets upon awaking. Their world is Tenebrae. They are the residents.

One such apparition, his name being Bordeaux, strides perfunctorily through the gnarled trees speckling the countryside. Aquiline of face, topped with a tangle of messy hair coloured to his namesake, Bordeaux carries with him an air of whimsy unmatched by that of the typecast demon. His skin is pale, hued white. His horns, violent as blood red, are small and curled as the twisted branches of the trees surrounding him. A burgundy coat is pulled taut across his narrow yet strong shoulders, which are hidden at times by the charcoal scarf draped about his collar. And as his fine black shoes crunched on the needles littering the forest floor, he turned his eyes skyward to observe the omnipresent canvas of night encompassing him. No moon shone at the present time, but it was no matter to Bordeaux. The years of darkness had left him with a seemingly enhanced vision. As such, a monochromatic gloom hung in the atmosphere, a tone of inescapable indifference.

Bordeaux's scarlet eyes squinted earnestly as his face contorted to a grimace. It was not the night that was troubling him but rather the heat wave that had enveloped the region of late. Seemingly unending, much like the night itself, the heat had sapped much of the demon's usual effervescent demeanor.

"Insufferable eternity!" he sighed, pressing a red silk handkerchief to his sweating temple before stuffing it back into his coat pocket.

His day had been a busy one. 'Day', it should be noted, referring solely upon twelve hours of time passing to where he stood now. For the forested regions of Tenebrae are shrouded in an everlasting blanket of midnight sky. Knowledge of such reasons surrounding this phenomenon trace their way back so far in time that they elude the present residents of Tenebrae Manor. Yet in spite of this, comprehension of an archaic magic spell has allowed remaining descendants to revivify the nightfall to a constant impenetrable strength. Yes, *why* the region is coated in night remains a mystery but the residents know that they *prefer* the darkness and choose to keep the spell active.

Bordeaux's hours had been stretched to their limits. His position in Tenebrae's walls as master of affairs was a most demanding vocation. However suiting it was to his pedantry, Bordeaux still found himself positively exhausted after the long hours working. And now, with the sudden arrival of a certain… guest, Bordeaux felt his frustration begin to overflow.

His spidery stride continued through the forest, steadily approaching the foot of the mountains. Out of the perpetual gloom before him a wooden hut manifested into view. Hearing his feet crunch on the pine needles, Bordeaux soon noticed another metronomic sound, namely that of steel splitting wood. As the hut came within reach, the demon slid his wispy hand along the log wall and circumnavigated it, shuddering at its splintery touch. And behind this hut a man came into view. Lean and muscular, two arms rose and fell, aimed and struck as an axe whirred down into the log chunk below, splitting like it was butter.

"Surely the firewood is unnecessary," said Bordeaux.

The man, not even flinching to the sudden appearance of a demon at his side, brushed his hands onto his green tunic. His face was coated in a fine film of sweat, dripping from his chestnut curls. "Bordeaux."

"Crow."

Crow nodded and scratched his scalp, the star-shaped ivy leaves which sprouted from a crudely made cap rustling. "Better to cut the logs now than leave it until the snows arrive."

His visitor began to pace casually in a semi-circle around the humble campsite. Crow had certainly set up a homely residence.

"They are saying things," said Crow.

Pondering a moment, Bordeaux replied, "Yes, I am aware."

"I heard this one's alive. More likely his sanity is on the decline but he lives."

"It has been an age since we last had a live one," said Bordeaux.

"I most definitely haven't met one. Or should I say, another."

"Ha! Hmm!" chuckled Bordeaux, "Yes, well, not all humans have your indifferent composure to the supernatural! Your decision to remain in this dusky locale bewilders me, then again, men are very strange creatures…"

Crow grinned. Mortal he was and comely for a youth in his third decade of life. Crow had assumed the role of a forest hermit, living under the black trees in a hut he had built himself.

"A human, yes. That is why I am here," explained Bordeaux.

Crow had resumed his wood chopping but continued to listen to the master of affairs.

"I have received reports regarding his arrival. And as I am yet to lay my eyes on him myself, I ponder whether you have any information this demon may find interesting."

"I had only a glimpse of him. Wandering through the trees, he was. He vanished from my sight quite quickly."

"And you thought not to engage a conversation with him?" Bordeaux inquired. "Surely the familiar face of man would have strengthened his resolve?"

Crow slouched his shoulders and let the axe swing at his side, "Bordeaux, you know I like to be left alone."

"Oh! Well pardon my intrusion!" the demon exclaimed, turning to walk away.

"No, wait!" called Crow. "Not you, the human. That is, I did not want to talk to him."

Bordeaux grinned.

"And no sooner than I'd seen him, I heard his cowardly scream off in the distance," the wood hermit continued.

"Hmm, yes. Well, I had heard of his arrival within the manor itself."

Crow's brows raised. "Bordeaux, within the manor?"

The demon nodded, hands clasped behind his back.

"Is he mad?"

"How am I to know?" said Bordeaux. "I was hoping you could divulge such information."

"I am not your messenger."

"No offense was intended," replied the demon. "It is just that I am so busy at present. Preparation and such."

Crow grinned. "He he, yes. The lady's birthday?"

Bordeaux nodded again, flicking a mote of dust from his burgundy coat. Another log split beneath the blow of Crow's axe, until the hermit hesitated.

"Were I in charge, I'd merely ignore the human's presence."

"Just so?"

"Yes. With the Lady Libra being so demanding, I'd be inclined to attend to her matters first. The human will deal with himself. In the end, they all die or go insane."

"And you, my dear Crow?" sniggered Bordeaux.

Crow smiled in return to the jest. The wood hermit seemed eager to induce Bordeaux's leave and he began to cut logs yet again. The crimson demon was not ignorant to his subtleties, though feeling somewhat deterred from his duties at the manor, remained idle within the campsite.

Bordeaux turned his gaze to a furnace glowing with embers, their dull glow reflecting off the iron braces strapped across a wooden shield that lay propped beside a stoker and bellows.

Approaching it almost cautiously, he peered lower to obtain closer inspection. It was a fine shield to be sure, a product of expert craftsmanship. Carved into the three-pronged star shape of a sycamore leaf, curled iron braces clung to its painted surface to create intricate venation. Dotted along said steel veins, glossy emeralds lay embedded.

"Why, Crow," Bordeaux gasped.

Crow had turned away from his axe work and was presently mopping the sweat from his brow. His visitor turned his head towards him. "Your work?"

Crow nodded.

"Magnificent."

"Just something I have been working on."

Bordeaux shook his head. "Quite remarkable and no doubt suitable for an apt swordsman such as yourself. Or perhaps it is intended for decorative purposes?"

"No, the former, Bordeaux."

The hermit became animated in a heartbeat, tossing the axe aside to present the fruits of his skills as a smith. He carefully picked up a lengthy strip of metal from the ground nearby and held it before him. "This, this is to be the sword to partner my masterpiece."

"Impressive," replied Bordeaux. "I have little reason to doubt it will be a spectacular weapon. I must interject though…"

"As to why?" Crow finished. "It is a precaution more than anything, I suppose. There have been more frequent sightings of Wood Golems recently."

"Ahh." Bordeaux hissed and rubbed his thumb and forefinger between his eyes. "More worriment."

"Slow creatures, Bordeaux. Slow of mind and stature. I would not let it concern you."

Bordeaux looked up and blinked with a sigh, "As you say, my dear Crow. I must ask you to be swift with your tempering of this weapon. For perhaps I may rely on you to keep these detestable things away from Tenebrae Manor?"

"I have enough to do about my own home."

The demon simpered in a way that made Crow grit his teeth.

"Don't be so coy, Bordeaux. If it pleases you, I will keep an eye out."

"There's a good lad."

Bordeaux and Crow stood erect and stared intently at each other for what seemed like several minutes, before the crimson demon broke their locked gaze, turned and took a step back towards his abode. Crow returned to the chopping block and, for a moment, the only sound was the crunch of their feet upon the fallen pine needles.

Bordeaux glanced over his shoulder. "Certainly, should you hear any more news of the human…"

"I will inform you immediately," Crow cut in. "But I'd say your fellow lodgers within the manor are likely to be more helpful."

"Indeed. Goodbye."

"Goodbye."

The splintering crush of dried conifer trunk beneath the cold blow of silver steel filled Bordeaux's pointed ears as he set out on his return journey. Shuffling his shoulders within his coat, the sweat enrapt him as he groaned in discomfort. The heat was certainly playing on his nerves. And now, these Wood Golems! What impropriety had Bordeaux done to deserve such anxieties? As he wandered through the forest, he slashed at a nearby tree trunk with his nails and hissed venomously through his teeth.

Tenebrae Manor loomed ahead out of the darkness, a macabre relic towering atop a small hill jutting from the jagged canopy. Bordeaux barely spared a glance at his immemorial home, too lost in his own reverie to enjoy the comforts of the dusky surroundings. Something was different. The demon could feel it in the atmosphere. Hidden amongst the suffocating heat, there was an unshakable feeling of foreboding, one that puzzled the fretful master of affairs.

Just as his mind began to turn back towards the tasks at hand, namely the birthday preparations for the mistress of the manor, his foot scuffed against a rough protuberance in the ground. He looked down in frustration at the interruption to observe a decayed shape crumble under his heel. One could be excused for thinking it merely an old tree branch or stump. But Bordeaux knew better of the surrounding regions and the creatures that lurked in the dark.

The creature in question at his feet was none other than a wood golem and its proximity to Tenebrae Manor only heightened his angst. The head, somewhat cylindrical and topped with dusty root like branches, had disintegrated significantly. It was most like that the creature had perished some time ago, for the bulging eyes of the thing had all but disappeared, leaving a pair of uneven hollows. Its body was indistinguishable from the soil about it, so decayed it was.

"So close to the house," muttered Bordeaux.

He kicked at the corpse, dislodging the head from it and sending it hurtling down the hill.

"Ah, I do not need this!" he repeated to himself. Surely Crow would be of some help to keep the golems at bay but their increased frequency was troubling Bordeaux. Deadly though these creatures were, the golems were so slow that they were usually destroyed before they could wrap their claws about the throats of their victims.

It was a favoured tactic of theirs, as some sick revenge for their own existence. They were essentially animated tree trunks, ripped from the ground by a noose and brought to life with the dark magic of a long-gone baron of Tenebrae. Bordeaux resumed his homeward stride, having formulated a plan of action in his mind. Yes, the golems could wait, if only for a moment. He had a celebration to plan and the mistress of the manor, the Lady Libra, was not wont to any form of patience or consideration.

The Will of the Wisp – Chapter 1

The following pages contain the first chapter of *The Will of the Wisp* – the second novel of P.S.Clinen.

The enigmatic hermit Mr. Wight has passed away, leaving his fortune to the estranged Mr. Fairlie. Mr. Pinnacle Tricks, Fairlie's assistant, is unceremoniously ushered off to Wight's isolated home in a Northern European forest to resolve the matter of the will. What begins as a routine task for Tricks quickly unravels into a mystery far bigger than he could have imagined. A love triangle, an unclaimed fortune, missing persons and ghostly sightings; nothing is what it seems and Tricks, an unwilling passenger to it all, must discover what is real and what is merely an illusion. A tangled tale of unspeakable betrayal and grudges left unforgiven, The Will of the Wisp is unique in its blend of drama, of horror, and the lengths people will go to protect who or what they love most.

Prologue - Ignis Fatuus

Savonia, Finland 1863

"Like cliffs which had been rent asunder; A dreary sea now flows between, But neither heat, nor frost, nor thunder, Shall wholly do away, I ween, The marks of that which once hath been."

- Samuel Taylor Coleridge

There was every indication of a storm brewing. The autumn, when the year is closest to death while still remaining alive – would be snuffed out by the coming storm. Vaporous vipers of mist coiled about the trees, adorning the cobwebbed forest. They hung from the branches; slithered over root and rotted leaves, gliding silently down the hillside until they slid over the surface of the slowly freezing lake, coating the land with death, clouding over the decay of plant matter that sighed upon the cold earth in soggy clumps. The emaciated branches clung desperately to the last of the leaves, although those star-shaped growths were long dead and shrivelled at the caress of late November wind; they would offer no further comfort. The lake ruffled under the skimming fingers of wind, and above, reflected and multiplied by the mirrored surface, thousands of small lights flickered like candles. They danced of their own accord, phantasmic and mysterious, though none could claim ownership of them. They were not fireflies. They were not the eyes of a myriad of beasts. Nor were they the oil lanterns of travellers on this ill-frequented forest path. The will-of-the-wisp - *ignis fatuus* - hovered like eldritch comets against the evening backdrop of the lake.

Accentuating the natural din of the forest, a certain foreign sound danced across the staff lines of the gale in pianissimo patters. Through the meditative rush of wind it was betrayed not by its volume, but rather the intrusiveness of such noise. A noise that did not belong in this wild scene - it was the roar of peoples. It was the thunderous clap of hooves. A fallen tree, hollowed out so that its rotted shell could offer sanctuary, housed the fearful huddle of a couple in hiding. They clung to one another, cursing the sharp breaths that escaped their lips in audible utterances - a concomitant of both cold and fright. The man cradled the woman as though she were a wounded bird, albeit his strong arms offered little warmth or protection from the elements, as such the both were wracked with shivers. He glanced at her dark head; wisps of black hair strung themselves over the florid beauty of her face, which presently upturned to his. Her eyes, of a piercingly beautiful green, betrayed the assailing fear that mounted in her breast. The look she gave belied the falsity of his confidence; a look that desperately implored that they had not pressed far enough into the forest to escape their predator. The man knew this to be true, and the fear of his mistress only further aggravated his composure. There was little he could do but accept that they were trapped.

He stifled a cough as the woman buried her head in the billows of his cloak. She looked up again, imploring, "The wind is wild! The trees are alive! Surely none would see us moving through the forest!"

Her urgent whisper hissed through the wind so that it was lost as soon as it was uttered; the man's heart lurched nonetheless, and he begged her silence. He did not respond immediately, but instead gazed out carefully from behind the tree to where the sky reddened above the canopy. He opened his mouth to speak, but the words choked in his throat and he cursed the audible baritone of his own murmurings, "The sun will soon set. It is then that we can make a move."

The woman said nothing, but the tear that streaked down her face was enough to shatter the man's heart and dash any intrepidness from his composure.

A skewbald stallion strode betwixt the birch boles. The pelt of the horse shone with an alpine white, splotched in various places with an autumnal auburn, giving it the very embodiment of the early winter forest through which it trotted. Its rider sat hunched and hollow, a ghostly husk atop saddle, drained of his mental energy. His eyes glazed with an unspeakable rage, a rage that increased with each passing second. He strained his ears, but the wind quite obviously impeded whatever it was he was listening for, and his face contorted to a grimacing snarl. Behind him, a small cavalry of horsemen followed obediently, faceless and sombre, as though they were mere trailing shadows of the first rider shifting with the fading light.

"We've but little time sir," one of them murmured, "The night will shield them."

"Don't you think I know that?" snapped the skewbald rider.

He wheeled his horse around with difficulty, the uneven forest floor proving troublesome. From beneath his wild, greying hair his gaze cut deep into his henchmen. It was a glare that they feared, a glare that spoke more than words ever could. Yet still he barked, "Find her. I do not care what it takes. I will have her returned!"

"Sir," came a cry, "what of the man?"

Here the skewbald rider flew into a rage, withdrawing his sword and aiming its blade skyward, "I care not what becomes of that devil! Let him die by your sword or by the unforgiving forest! Just return *her* to me!"

The men dispersed, taking unique paths through the trees, while the skewbald rider steadied his stallion and again cursed through his teeth.

The woman sobbed wretchedly from the shelter of the fallen tree. She watched as the man crept out from their hiding spot and surveyed the surroundings. He turned back to her with a new vigour in his determination.

"We need to make for the lake. If we can get there unseen, their horses will not be able to travel down the steep embankment."

"Could he have assumed us to have made further ground?"

"That is what I am hoping. Come."

Fighting against the trembling in her legs, she arose and followed him into the trees.

Having lost sight of his men, the skewbald rider continued down the sodden path. The forest oozed with damp; the freezing moisture dripping from the trees like cold sweat, while the ground beneath his horse's hooves shifted as they struggled on.

She surely cannot have gotten far in these conditions, not without a horse or provisions.

He cursed the wind as it cut coldly into him. About his body drifted a vibrant vigour; truly the forest was alive. Through the trees, he could see the sludge-like surface of the lake some distance down the hill, and cursed the ghost lights that appeared in the corners of his vision. Those mischievous fairies of luminance gave the impression of the torches of wandering travellers; he vehemently hoped one of them would illuminate his renegade wife. But each floating mote of light that met his gaze brought nothing with it, only adding fuel to his fury.

Curse those lights!

He would then shoot to attention, for from a distance came an otherworldly holler. A shiver rattled down his spine, and it would take the skewbald rider a few seconds to comprehend the cry was not that of some eldritch beast, but rather a twofold bellow of man and horse. Had his wife been found? The stallion was kicked briskly into a gallop, its hoof claps underlining its nervous braying, for the trees were close and the ground uneven. More voices began to permeate in the forest, and for a moment the rider would again feel a mysterious uneasiness. Something sinister seemed to lurk in the trees, an unseen charlatan of mischief that had the rider's blood going cold. But no, it could not be a phantom - those voices indeed belonged to his men, confirmed to him as he entered a small clearing where the cavalry was huddled around a thrashing mass of cloth and flesh. Dismounting, he brandished his whip and moved towards them.

"Stand aside!" he barked, "At last…"

But he would not see that which he desired. Below the party of horsemen lay a crippled mare that complained in a sickening whinny, its rider pinned painfully beneath its girth.

So this is what made that awful moan.

"A rabbit warren, sir," said one of the men, "she caught her foot in it."

"You mean you have not found *her* yet?"

"N-no sir. Nowhere to be seen, and we must turn back to the house! This pair needs attention and the sun is all but gone!"

"I'll have you all freeze to death before we turn back. We are not turning back until my wife is recovered!"

"Sir," cried another man, "I beg you to reconsider. We -"

"Get the man out from beneath that animal."

The fallen rider, a young boy only recently of age, limped gingerly on his leg, bracing himself against his comrades while the mare continued to groan on the ground. Before the men could react, the skewbald rider snatched his blunderbuss and shot the beast, instantly silencing it.

"Sir!"

The astonished riders gaped, instantly taken aback. The clumsy weapon had been enough to snuff out the life of the injured horse, the eyes of the men dropping as their leader glared at each of them one by one.

"Find her."

From the edge of the clearing the crows scattered; black wing beats pounded the air, and through the tousle of midnight feathers the skewbald rider saw what he was looking for. Those eyes, those incomparable green eyes stared fixedly upon him; fear rooting the woman to the spot. In a second both were running. The rider trailed his renegade wife with cumbersome steps, the heavy blunderbuss his burden. Amongst the branches that brushed against his face as he ran he could discern another figure - his old friend, his betrayer.

So it is as I feared.

He pursued the couple desperately, the treble struggling with the elements that pressed on them at all sides. The wind roared, the branches whipped and struck, the mud shifted beneath their hurried flight. They rumbled down the hill with reckless abandon, the trio locked in a futile stalemate where neither party was advancing upon or moving further towards escape.

"Harlot!" roared the pursuer, "Cease this amour! You would forsake me? You would forsake your children?!"

Bursting onto the lakeside, the renegade man tripped and slid painfully across the thick ice that coated the surface. His attacker wasted no time in leaping upon him, at last realising the uselessness of his lumbering blunderbuss and withdrawing instead a small dagger from his belt. The two men fought on the ice, hurling their fists in a flurry of primal fury. The ice groaned as both men were slammed into the frozen surface in the struggle. Yet despite his blind focus upon his abhorred rival, neither man would be deaf to the tiny cry that escaped the blue lips of the woman they fought for. Still clasping at each other's collars, they turned to where she had slid further from the shore onto the ice shelf. Both had not realised the extent of their brawl sending an ominous fissure between her and the safety of the shore, and now all that accompanied the wind's howl was the blood-curdling crack of splitting ice. For a second that seemingly lasted for an eternity the treble was frozen in fear, the woman's eyes bulging with awful terror, before at last the horrible groan of the ice grew louder and she was plunged into the inky lake water. Her scream would only sound for a moment before it was smothered by the frigid needles of the tarn, while her husband and lover could only watch in horror as the prize of their jealously was lost beneath the darkness of the lake. Above the wind came the very same moan heard earlier by her husband, though perhaps it was merely the trickery of the foreboding nature surrounding. For when both men were able to wrest their eyes from that wretched spot - that black pool that intruded upon flawless ice - they could observe the ignis fatuus, the eyes of the will-o-the-wisp staring down upon their treachery.

About the author:

P.S.Clinen lives in New South Wales, Australia. He has written two novels and hopes to have a third completed one day. All of his works can be found online.

Check out more at psclinen.com

www.ingramcontent.com/pod-product-compliance
Lightning Source LLC
Chambersburg PA
CBHW050954050426
42337CB00051B/1089